A Guide to Executing Change for Executive Leaders

Participant Workbook

Wayne R. Davis

T0345117

Pfeiffer

A Wiley Imprint

www.pfeiffer.com

Published by Pfeiffer
An Imprint of Wiley
989 Market Street, San Francisco, CA 94103-1741
www.pfeiffer.com

For additional copies/bulk purchases of this book in the U.S. please contact 800-274-4434.

Pfeiffer books and products are available through most bookstores. To contact Pfeiffer directly call our Customer Care Department within the U.S. at 800-274-4434, outside the U.S. at 317-572-3985, fax 317-572-4002, or visit www.pfeiffer.com.

Pfeiffer also publishes its books in a variety of electronic formats. Some content that appears in print may not be available in electronic books.

Executive Leaders: Participant Workbook ISBN: 978-0-470-40004-3

Acquiring Editor: Holly Allen
Marketing Manager: Tolu Babalola
Director of Development: Kathleen Dolan Davies
Developmental Editor: Susan Rachmeler
Production Editor: Michael Kay
Editor: Rebecca Taff
Assistant Editor: Marisa Kelley
Manufacturing Supervisor: Becky Morgan

Printed in the United States of America

Printing   10 9 8 7 6 5 4 3 2 1

Contents

1. Establishing Guidelines and Assigning Accountability   1

2. Identifying the Key Outcomes, Strategies, Initiatives, and Business Objectives   7

3. Articulating the Compelling Message   17

4. Change Readiness Assessment   23

5. Change Risk Assessment   31

6. Change Style Assessment   41

Establishing Guidelines and Assigning Accountability

FOR THIS EXERCISE, you'll be discussing the questions below as a full group. Record your response to each question in the space allotted.

Identify Candidates for Key Change Roles

Who will be responsible for determining the desired **outcomes** of the transformation?	
Why is this person(s) the best choice?	
What unique capabilities or competencies does this person(s) bring?	
Because of this new and added responsibility, will the person(s) need to shift some present workload? How will this be done?	
Does this person(s) have significant change management experience? If not, discuss how you will address this issue.	

Who will have the delegated authority to refine the desired **outcomes**?	
Why is this person(s) the best choice?	
What unique capabilities or competencies does this person(s) bring?	
Because of this new and added responsibility, will the person(s) need to shift some present workload? How will this be done?	
Does this person(s) have significant change management experience? If not, discuss how you will address this issue.	

Who is responsible for constructing the change **strategy** and roadmap?	
Why is this person(s) the best choice?	
What unique capabilities or competencies does this person(s) bring?	
Because of this new and added responsibility, will the person(s) need to shift some present workload? How will this be done?	
Does this person(s) have significant change management experience? If not, discuss how you will address this issue.	

Who oversees and course corrects the change **strategy**?	
Why is this person(s) the best choice?	
What unique capabilities or competencies does this person(s) bring?	
Because of this new and added responsibility, will the person(s) need to shift some present workload? How will this be done?	
Does this person(s) have significant change management experience? If not, discuss how you will address this issue.	

Who will prioritize and integrate the **change initiatives**?	
Why is this person(s) the best choice?	
What unique capabilities or competencies does this person(s) bring?	
Because of this new and added responsibility, will the person(s) need to shift some present workload? How will this be done?	
Does this person(s) have significant change management experience? If not, discuss how you will address this issue.	

Who will design and develop the **change processes**?	
Why is this person(s) the best choice?	
What unique capabilities or competencies does this person(s) bring?	
Because of this new and added responsibility, will the person(s) need to shift some present workload? How will this be done?	
Does this person(s) have significant change management experience? If not, discuss how you will address this issue.	

Who is responsible for the **alignment** of the initiatives and change processes as the overall effort develops?	
Why is this person(s) the best choice?	
What unique capabilities or competencies does this person(s) bring?	
Because of this new and added responsibility, will the person(s) need to shift some present workload? How will this be done?	
Does this person(s) have significant change management experience? If not, discuss how you will address this issue.	

Who is responsible for determining the project **resource requirements**?	
Why is this person(s) the best choice?	
What unique capabilities or competencies does this person(s) bring?	
Because of this new and added responsibility, will the person(s) need to shift some present workload? How will this be done?	
Does this person(s) have significant change management experience? If not, discuss how you will address this issue.	

Who is accountable for overseeing the project's **budget and reporting**?	
Why is this person(s) the best choice?	
What unique capabilities or competencies does this person(s) bring?	
Because of this new and added responsibility, will the person(s) need to shift some present workload? How will this be done?	
Does this person(s) have significant change management experience? If not, discuss how you will address this issue.	

Who is the person responsible for overall project **status reporting**?	
Why is this person(s) the best choice?	
What unique capabilities or competencies does this person(s) bring?	
Because of this new and added responsibility, will the person(s) need to shift some present workload? How will this be done?	
Does this person(s) have significant change management experience? If not, discuss how you will address this issue.	

Who will establish and oversee the **roles and responsibilities** of the change management team and the change process owners (managers)?	
Why is this person(s) the best choice?	
What unique capabilities or competencies does this person(s) bring?	
Because of this new and added responsibility, will the person(s) need to shift some present workload? How will this be done?	
Does this person(s) have significant change management experience? If no, discuss how you will address this issue.	

Who owns and makes the **key change decisions** affecting change strategy, initiatives, and processes?	
Why is this person(s) the best choice?	
What unique capabilities or competencies does this person(s) bring?	
Because of this new and added responsibility, will the person(s) need to shift some present workload? How will this be done?	
Does this person(s) have significant change management experience? If no, discuss how you will address this issue.	

Notes

Identifying the Key Outcomes, Strategies, Initiatives, and Business Objectives

NOW YOU WILL identify your key outcomes, strategies, initiatives, and business objectives.

Key Outcomes

Complete the following worksheet by considering the desired outcomes of the change transformation. List four outcomes that define the success of the change.

Examples

Outcome 1. A workforce model measured by agility, responsiveness, and competence

Outcome 2. A business model measured by growth, cost containment, and performance

Outcome 3. A cultural environment measured by innovation, creativity, and speed

Outcome 4. A service delivery model measured by quality, connectivity, and reputation

---

Outcomes Worksheet

Outcome 1

Outcome 2

Outcome 3

Outcome 4

Discussion Questions

As a whole group, you'll report out your outcomes and select five key desired outcomes. For each of the selected outcomes, discuss:

- Who is responsible for achieving this outcome?

- How will you know you have achieved the desired results?

- What are the potential roadblocks or work-arounds you need to think about?

- If you miss the target, what is the impact going forward?

Key Strategies

What are the key strategies needed to accomplish the change? Complete the next worksheet by listing four strategies in rank order of importance to the success of the change initiative. Some examples follow.

Sample Strategies

Conduct Business Diagnostic
An internal self-assessment of the essential qualities to conduct business such as market segmentation, core competencies, critical success factors, strengths, weaknesses, and an assessment of leadership, culture, technology and business systems, innovation, performance metrics, and operational standards and practices.

Assess Current Markets
Conduct an assessment of current markets, industry breadth and scope, key buyer values, supplier influence and leverage, intensity of competition, and industry attractiveness.

Analyze Emerging Markets and Trends
Identify and understand emerging market dynamics, change drivers, economic conditions, future market scenarios, and potential market opportunities and their convergence.

Define and Analyze Competitive Position
Identify sources of competitive advantage, summarize competitive strengths and weaknesses, and define competitive positioning within future market environments.

Key Strategies Worksheet

Strategy 1

Strategy 2

Strategy 3

Strategy 4

What was your logic and rationale in ranking the strategies?

Discussion

As a whole group, you'll report out your strategies and select three key strategies. For each of the selected strategies, discuss:

- How will we align the organization with the strategy?
- Who is responsible for executing or implementing the strategy?

Key Initiatives

What are the key change initiatives? An initiative is a broad area of focus that can encompass a single project or many projects. Complete this worksheet by listing four initiatives that will assure successful change. A few examples follow.

Examples

Many times business initiatives revolve around a single or multiple projects. If you are finding it difficult to identify individual change initiatives, start by listing the present and/or anticipated projects associated with the change. Next, group these projects into similar categories and define them as a change initiative.

Typically, change initiatives focus on creating value, leveraging synergies, exploiting technologies, containing costs, operating more efficiently and effectively, maximizing revenues, recruiting, developing, and retaining talent, acquiring strategic assets, and improving outcomes and satisfaction.

Key Initiatives Worksheet

Change Initiative 1

Change Initiative 2

Change Initiative 3

Change Initiative 4

Discussion

As a whole group, you'll report out your initiatives and select the four that you believe are most important. For each of the selected initiatives, discuss:

- Who is responsible and accountable for this initiative?
- What resources do they need? budget? people? tools?
- What metrics, indicators, and measurements are needed to track progress?

Key Business Objectives

What are the key business objectives? Complete this worksheet by defining four business objectives: one each at the strategic level, the business unit level, the department or functional level, and the team, workgroup, or individual contributor level. Some examples follow.

Examples

Strategic objectives (from the organization's strategic plan)

- Market leadership
- Technical superiority
- Financial performance

Business unit objectives (from defined performance goals)

- Grow sales
- Contain costs
- Improve service
- Operational excellence

Department or functional objectives (from functional department mandates)

- Talent development
- Interpersonal effectiveness
- Collaborative relationships

Team, work group, or individual contributor objectives (from task assignment and accomplishment)

- Task accomplishment
- Interpersonal communication
- Intra-team effectiveness

Key Business Objectives

1. Strategic objective:

2. Business unit objective:

3. Department or functional objective:

4. Team, workgroup, or individual contributor objective:

Discussion

As a whole group, you'll report out your objectives. Then you'll select two objectives that you believe will have the greatest impact for each category.

Notes

_____

_____

_____

_____

_____

_____

_____

_____

_____

_____

_____

_____

_____

_____

_____

_____

_____

_____

3

Articulating the Compelling Message

COMPLETE THIS EXERCISE by developing a key word list, writing benefit statements, and using the knowledge gained to write a well articulated change statement.

Individual Activity: Develop a Key Word List

List a total of five words you feel define the expectations of the change.

1.

2.

3.

4.

5.

Examples	
Leverage	Launch
Strength	Recognition
Flexibility	Brand
Talent	Uncharted
Competence	Apart
Breakthrough	Engage

Group Activity: Refine the Word List

Share your word list with the other participants. Group the collective words by similarity. Rank the list of words by their ability to convey the meaning and essence of the change. Select the five words that you will emphasize to articulate the change message.

1.

2.

3.

4.

5.

Group Activity: Create Benefit Statements

Complete this activity by answering each of the questions below with a benefit statement. Add two additional benefit statements you feel are appropriate for each category.

People	Benefit Statement
How will the change initiative make this a great place to work?	
How will the change initiative reinforce our values system?	
How will the change initiative promote a culture of learning?	
1.	
2.	

Organization	Benefit Statement
How will the change initiative improve our image?	
How will the change initiative increase our competitiveness?	
How will the change initiative help us serve customers better?	
1.	
2.	

Group Activity: Create a Change Statement

Using the word list from earlier in this exercise, write a brief and well-articulated statement (not more than two sentences) that encompasses and expresses the core meaning of the change initiative. Be concise, succinct, and complete, so that when read, the reader will have a holistic and contextual understanding of the change.

Several examples of change statements are shown below.

Examples of Typical Change Statements

The outcome of our change initiative will engage our customers in a new "brand experience." This experience of innovative media, immersive audio, and inspirational design will set us apart and launch a new era in an exciting, uncharted market space for our organization.

This change initiative, when implemented, will allow us to refocus our efforts on providing our customers with effective and affordable products and services by:

- Performing research, marketing, logistics, and support services

- Applying our unique technologies and solutions

- Engaging a workforce recognized for operational excellence

- Providing our stakeholders an opportunity to share our success through growth, reward, and profit

---

Your Change Statement

1.

2.

Group Activity: Write a Change Communication Statement

Next, using the results of previous activities, complete the worksheet below, which will serve as the project announcement to your employees. If you have already communicated the message to your employees, adapt and complete the worksheet for announcing the project to your customers, your community, or as a PR release to your local newspaper.

Change Communication	
Objective	
Theme	
Visuals and Graphics	
Text	
Invite Feedback and Input	
Additional Information	

Notes

4

Change Readiness Assessment

NOW IT'S TIME TO DETERMINE your readiness for change.

Overview

This Change Readiness Assessment provides an opportunity for you to determine the readiness for change and identifies four areas of readiness: Organization, Individual, Culture, and Technical.

Instructions

The Change Readiness Assessment consists of twenty questions in the form of agreement statements. You complete the assessment by circling the number that corresponds with your perception of how the statement characterizes your organization.

See the following example before you begin. Please answer every question. Do not leave any question unanswered.

Example	
Change Readiness Assessment	**Do You Agree?** **Circle One**
Organization	
1. The organization's leadership has the buy-in and will provide the sponsorship backing for this change initiative.	Not at All .... Very Much 1-------2----③-----4------5

Change Readiness Assessment	Do You Agree? Circle One
Organization	
1. The organization's leadership has the buy-in and will provide the sponsorship backing for this change initiative.	Not at All .... Very Much 1-------2-------3-------4-------5
2. The implementation of this change initiative is very important to middle management.	Not at All .... Very Much 1-------2-------3-------4-------5
3. Leadership has communicated a consistent message about the benefits of this change initiative.	Not at All .... Very Much 1-------2-------3-------4-------5
4. The organization has the skills and competencies to implement this change initiative.	Not at All .... Very Much 1-------2-------3-------4-------5
5. Employees have the motivation required to complete this change initiative.	Not at All .... Very Much 1-------2-------3-------4-------5
6. Management has articulated how people will be rewarded for supporting this change initiative.	Not at All .... Very Much 1-------2-------3-------4-------5
7. Customers are well informed of this change initiative and are positively onboard.	Not at All .... Very Much 1-------2-------3-------4-------5
8. Management has presented a compelling case how work processes will improve as a result of this change initiative.	Not at All .... Very Much 1-------2-------3-------4-------5

Circle the number that corresponds with your perception of how the statement characterizes your personal feeling toward change and the subject change initiative.

Change Readiness Assessment	Do You Agree? Circle One
Individual	
9. I see this change initiative providing increased opportunity for me and my job growth.	Not at All .... Very Much 1-------2-------3-------4-------5
10. I am confident I will get the training I need to be a successful contributor to this change initiative.	Not at All .... Very Much 1-------2-------3-------4-------5
11. I am confident I and others will be recognized and rewarded for doing a good job on this change initiative.	Not at All .... Very Much 1-------2-------3-------4-------5
12. I am confident the managers and front-line supervisors will provide the direction needed.	Not at All .... Very Much 1-------2-------3-------4-------5

Circle the number that corresponds with your perception of how the statement characterizes the culture in your organization.

Change Readiness Assessment	Do You Agree? Circle One
Culture	
13. The organization has a successful track record implementing similar change initiatives.	Not at All .... Very Much 1-------2-------3-------4-------5
14. The organization has a high level of stick-to-it-ness and will not bend or snap under pressure.	Not at All .... Very Much 1-------2-------3-------4-------5
15. There is a clear alignment between the organization's business goals and this change initiative.	Not at All .... Very Much 1-------2-------3-------4-------5

16. The organization's value statements are well aligned with and will not be compromised by the new change.	Not at All .... Very Much 1-------2-------3-------4-------5
17. The organization will be able to keep its unique individualism after the change is implemented.	Not at All .... Very Much 1-------2-------3-------4-------5

Circle the number that corresponds with your perception of how the statement characterizes your view of the technical infrastructure and staff in your organization.

Change Readiness Assessment	Do You Agree? Circle One
Technical	
18. The technical infrastructure is capable of absorbing the added pressures resulting from the change initiative.	Not at All .... Very Much 1-------2-------3-------4-------5
19. The technical staff is competent and understands the importance and impact of this change.	Not at All .... Very Much 1-------2-------3-------4-------5
20. The technical staff has successfully implemented major change initiatives of this magnitude and dimension in the past.	Not at All .... Very Much 1-------2-------3-------4-------5

Change Readiness Scoring Sheet

Referring to your response to the questions on the assessment, enter the value of the number you circled in the appropriate space and column below. Then sum each column and enter the score in the Total box.

Number	Organization	Individual	Culture	Technical
1.				
2.				
3.				
4.				
5.				
6.				
7.				
8.				
9.				
10.				
11.				
12.				
13.				
14.				
15.				
16.				
17.				
18.				
19.				
20.				
Total				

Change Readiness Results

Next, divide the Organization total by 8 and circle the number that most closely represents your result.

Organization Total/8

| Not at All .... Very Much |
| 1-------2-------3-------4-------5 |

Divide the Individual total by 4 and circle the number that most closely represents your result.

Individual Total/4

| Not at All .... Very Much |
| 1-------2-------3-------4-------5 |

Divide the Culture total by 5 and circle the number that most closely represents your result.

Culture Total/5

| Not at All .... Very Much |
| 1-------2-------3-------4-------5 |

Divide the Technical total by 3 and circle the number that most closely represents your result.

Technical Total/3

| Not at All .... Very Much |
| 1-------2-------3-------4-------5 |

Change Readiness Issue Areas

Count the responses you circled as either "1" or "2" on the Assessment. Check the box below that corresponds to your count.

- ☐   0 to 5 = Smooth road ahead
- ☐   6 to 10 = Some bumps and curves ahead
- ☐   11 to 15 = Some major roadblocks ahead
- ☐   16 to 20 = Some critical road closures and detours ahead

How would you propose to overcome or neutralize the issues you circled as either "1" or "2"?

_____

_____

_____

_____

_____

Arrange in rank order, where 1 is the most important readiness issue to address and 4 is the least important readiness issue to address, for your organization.

_____ Organization Readiness

_____ Individual Readiness

_____ Culture Readiness

_____ Technical Readiness

Notes

5

Change Risk Assessment

THIS CHANGE RISK Assessment provides an opportunity for you to determine the risk, obstacles, barriers, and complexity for a change initiative.

Overview

The Change Risk Assessment consists of eighteen questions related to risk, four on obstacles and barriers, and eight on complexity. You conduct the assessment by answering the questions according to your perception of how the statements characterize your organization.

The seven risk components in this assessment include:

- Political
- Technology
- Cultural
- Financial
- Image
- Customer
- Know-How

The six obstacles and barriers components in this assessment include:

- Timeline
- Resources
- Commitment
- Resistance
- Two write-ins

The eight complexity components in this assessment include:

- Speed
- Disruption
- Direction
- Dimension
- Uncertainty
- Familiarization
- Dependency
- Political

Instructions

Each of the three components of this assessment has its own instructions and scoring, which the facilitator will review with you. When working through this assessment, please answer every question. Do not leave any question unanswered.

Project Risks

Complete this portion of the assessment by reading each statement and checking the column that indicates your perception. *Note:* Please be aware that Columns 1 and 2 contain some reversed labels of "Yes" and "No."

Change Risk Assessment

Risks	1	2

Political	No	Yes
1. The political power factor is an issue in our organization and is exacerbated by top-down decision making and a command-and-control mentality.		
2. Counter-productive, and even bad or wrong decisions, are slow to be corrected.		
3. Reputation has it that in our company, advancement is by "who you know" not "what you know."		

Technology	No	Yes
4. With new projects, IT in our organization is generally over-optimistic.		
5. With new projects, IT in our organization has a reputation of schedule slide.		
6. With new projects, IT in our organization often complains about "feature creep."		

Cultural	Yes	No
7. Our people know our value system and generally follow it in conducting business.		
8. We're aware right away when there is a value shift that will reflect negatively on the organization.		
9. When confronted with heavy time demands, we insist our employees maintain a healthy work/life balance.		

Financial	No	Yes
10. Management's "pet" projects are rarely consolidated, reevaluated, or cancelled.		
11. Resource allocation is traditionally based on a "favorite son" lineup.		

Image	Yes	No
12. When consolidation or downsizing is required, we have a plan in place that assures people's dignity and self-worth.		
13. We do whatever it takes to maintain our "company of choice" image.		

Risks	1	2

Customer	Yes	No
14. We regularly invite customers to be members of our planning, product development, and cost-containment teams.		
15. We currently have a plan in place that will monitor the affects of this change initiative on our customers.		

Know-How	No	Yes
16. We tend to rely on our own expertise and are not convinced that third parties bring much value to the table.		
17. We encourage the opinions of others, but generally act on ideas put forth by the senior staff.		
18. Our workforce as a whole is very good at what they do, but they don't understand the business in the same way as the senior staff.		
Add the number of checks in each column and enter the totals here. TOTAL		
Calculate the percentages in each column by dividing the total for each column by 18. PERCENT*		

*If the percentage of 2s is 20 percent or higher, that is an indicator of potential roadblocks occurring during the change process. Remember, all items checked in Column 2 are opportunities for improvement.

Obstacles and Barriers Assessment

Conduct this assessment by writing responses to the question posed in each category. Please add two additional obstacles and/or barriers and your response in the space provided below.

Timeline

How will you deal with compressed timelines?

Resources

How will you address the issue of an inadequate budget?

Commitment

How will you confront unenthusiastic commitment?

Resistance

How will you turn resistance to change into a positive force?

1.

2.

Complexity Assessment

Complete this assessment by reading each statement and circling the number in the scale box according to how you perceive the statement characterizes your situation.

Complexity and Risk of Change			
1. Speed of change. How fast will the change be?	We will fall behind.	We will keep up.	We will stay ahead.
	0 .... 25 .... 50 .... 75 100		
2. Disruption of change. How much chaos will it create?	Chaos will abound.	Some disruption	Little/no disruption
	0 .... 25 .... 50 .... 75 100		
3. Direction of change. How far out of our comfort zone?	Brand new road ahead	Familiar, some detours	Well-traveled road
	0 .... 25 .... 50 .... 75 100		
4. Dimension of change. How deep will the change go?	Will touch all	Will touch many	Will touch few
	0 .... 25 .... 50 .... 75 100		
5. Uncertainty of change. How good are we at changing?	We're not very good at change.	We've gone through similar change.	We've got a lot of experience.
	0 .... 25 .... 50 .... 75 100		
6. Uncharted water of change. How familiar are we with where we're headed?	We're in over our heads.	We can tread water and get our bearings.	We're good swimmers.
	0 .... 25 .... 50 .... 75 100		
7. Dependency factors. Do we have control of all of the parts?	We will depend heavily on others.	We have control of some but not all major parts.	Everything is entirely within our control.
	0 .... 25 .... 50 .... 75 100		
8. Political factors. Is everyone on board?	There are skeptics and doubters.	A lot of wait-and-see.	There is substantial buy-in.
	0 .... 25 .... 50 .... 75 100		

Complexity of Change

Record the value (0, 25, 50, 75, 100) you gave for each statement in the appropriate spaces below.

1	
2	
3	
4	
5	
6	
7	
8	
Add the numbers in the second column and enter the grand total here.	

Discussion

What single component or factor in the assessment do you feel is the most impacting on your organization?

Why?

What additional components of complexity and risk do you feel should be included for your organization?

Notes

6

Change Style Assessment

THE CHANGE STYLE ASSESSMENT is the next step in the process.

Overview

The Change Style Assessment provides an opportunity for you to determine your unique "change style." You identify your style by responding to twenty-one questions; the grouping of your answers will indicate with which style you most closely identify.

Instructions

The Change Style Assessment consists of twenty-one questions. You complete the assessment using sentence completion and checking the phrase that best describes you.

Please answer every question. Do not leave any question unanswered.

If you have difficulty selecting a single answer, ask yourself which response would be most natural or likely for you at work.

There are no *wrong answers* to these questions, so base your response on how you are today, not how you think you should be or would like to be in the future.

Example

1. When planning change, I want to know . . .

    a. *What do we need to do to be competitive?*

✗ b. *What people needs are being considered?*

    c. *What has worked in the past?*

    d. *What opportunities will the change create?*

Change Style Assessment

1. When planning change, I want to know . . .

____a. What do we need to do to be competitive?

____b. What people needs are being considered?

____c. What has worked in the past?

____d. What opportunities will the change create?

2. If an important decision is to be made, I . . .

____a. Think it through completely before deciding.

____b. Go with my gut instincts.

____c. Consider the impact it will have on other people before deciding.

____d. Run it by someone whose opinion I respect before deciding.

3. During change, I want to know . . .

____a. How will the change affect people?

____b. Who is committed to the change?

____c. Why are we making the change?

____d. What needs to be done?

4. If I am having a conflict with a co-worker or customer, I . . .

____a. Try to help the situation along by focusing on the positive.

____b. Stay calm and try to understand the cause of the conflict.

____c. Try to avoid discussing the issue causing the conflict.

____d. Confront it right away so that it can bet resolved as soon as possible.

5. My preferred role during change is to . . .

____a. Take charge.

____b. Build consensus.

____c. Work behind the scenes.

____d. Pay attention to the details.

6. My motto is . . .

____a. "Don't speak ill of boss or colleagues."

____b. "Let's do it right, no matter what it takes."

____c. "Don't bug me with rules, limits, and details."

____d. "Let's get it done and get it done now."

7. I approach change . . .

____a. With caution: "Is this just another change for change's sake?"

____b. As necessary to achieve goals.

____c. With enthusiasm for new opportunities.

____d. With concern about how the change will affect responsibilities, relationships and culture

8. The word that most accurately describes me during change is . . .

____a. Persuasive.

____b. Cautious.

____c. Loyal.

____d. Commanding.

9. When a co-worker or customer is explaining a problem to me, I . . .

____a. Try to understand and empathize with how he or she is feeling.

____b. Look for the specific facts pertaining to the situation.

____c. Listen carefully for the main issue so that I can find a solution.

____d. Use my body language and tone of voice to show her or him that I understand.

10. When attending training programs or presentations, I . . .

____a. Become bored if the person moves too slowly.

____b. Try to be supportive of the speaker, knowing how hard the job is.

____c. Want it to be entertaining as well as informative.

____d. Look for the logic behind what the speaker is saying.

11. When I want to put my point across to others, I . . .

____a. Listen to the individual's point of view first and then express my ideas gently.

____b. Strongly state my opinion so that person knows where I stand.

____c. Try to persuade him or her without being too forceful.

____d. Explain the thinking and logic behind what I am saying.

12. It is important for me to know . . .

____a. What is the realistic reason for the change?

____b. What is expected of me personally?

____c. What has to be accomplished?

____d. Will I be involved with new people, ideas and initiatives?

13. I set goals and objectives at work that I . . .

____a. Think I can realistically attain.

____b. Feel are challenging and would be exciting to achieve.

____c. Need to achieve as part of a bigger objective.

____d. Think will make me feel good when I achieve them.

14. When explaining a problem to a co-worker from whom I need help, I . . .

____a. Explain the problem in as much detail as possible.

____b. Sometimes exaggerate to make my point.

____c. Try to explain how the problem makes me feel.

____d. Explain how I would like the problem to be solved.

15. Words that best describe me are . . .

____a. Outgoing, enthusiastic, and creative.

____b. Diplomatic, dependable, and sensitive.

____c. Serious, quiet, and business-like.

____d. Decisive, forceful, and blunt.

16. When I am behind on a project and feel pressure to get it done, I . . .

____a. Make a list of everything I need to do, in what order, by when.

____b. Block out everything else and focus 100 percent on the work I need to do.

____c. Become anxious and have a hard time focusing on my work.

____d. Set a deadline to complete the project and do it.

17. When I feel verbally attacked by a customer or a co-worker, I . . .

____a. Tell the person to stop.

____b. Feel hurt but usually don't say anything about it to him or her.

____c. Ignore her or his anger and try to focus on the facts of the situation.

____d. Let the person know in strong terms that I don't like his or her behavior.

18. I am most interested in . . .

____a. A warm social environment with secure working conditions where my loyalty and teaming skills are valued.

____b. A predictable environment with set rules and procedures where I can use my logic and diagnostic skills.

____c. An environment that is constantly changing, where I can affect growth, efficiency, and production.

____d. A friendly, collaborative environment where I can use my creative and social skills to benefit the company.

19. My communication style is . . .

____a. Fast-paced, enthusiastic, big-picture oriented.

____b. Business-focused, to-the-point, authoritative.

____c. Personal, soft spoken, good listener.

____d. Formal, structured, facts, and detail focused.

20. What is important to me is . . .

____a. Job security, cooperation, and approval.

____b. No surprises, ample resources, and alone time.

____c. Challenging goals, control, and power.

____d. Variety, new possibilities, and flexibility.

21. What I can do to be more effective is . . .

____a. Take more risks, decide faster, and monitor my perfectionism.

____b. Look before I leap, improve my time management, and be more objective.

____c. Disagree when necessary, develop greater assertiveness, and be more open to change.

____d. Ask, listen more, and monitor my high expectation of self and others.

Scoring

Referring to your responses to the questions on the Change Style Assessment, circle the appropriate letter that corresponds to your answer to each question.

Question Number	Collaborator	Protector	Initiator	Questioner
1	d	b	a	c
2	d	c	b	a
3	b	a	d	c
4	a	b	d	c
5	b	c	a	d
6	c	a	d	b
7	c	d	b	a
8	a	c	d	b
9	d	a	c	b
10	c	b	a	d
11	c	a	b	d
12	d	b	c	a
13	b	d	c	a
14	b	c	d	a
15	a	b	d	c
16	d	c	b	a
17	d	b	a	c
18	d	a	c	b
19	a	c	b	d
20	d	a	c	b
21	b	c	d	a
Total				

Now count the number of letters you circled in each column and record the answer in the appropriate box. To verify your work, the sum of the four boxes should be equal to 21.

Your highest score indicates the style you most closely identify with.

As a group, you'll find the total number of participants who identify with each style. You'll also calculate the percentage each style comprises of the group overall.

Collaborator	Protector	Initiator	Questioner
Count:	Count:	Count:	Count:
Percentage:	Percentage:	Percentage:	Percentage:

Change Style Map

Change Role: Preferred role during change
Orientation: Focus during change
Openness to Change: Attitude about change
Emotional Expression: Degree of emotion expressed during change

Change Style Profiles

	Collaborator
Characteristics	

Characteristics

Assertive, confident and outgoing

Visionaries who focus on new possibilities

Excited and optimistic about change

Contributions During Change

Use creative talents and social skills to build good personal relationships that will benefit the company

Excels at introducing and gaining buy-in for change

Comfortable with ambiguity; can see both sides of an issue

Needs During Change

Help with organization, structure, schedules and deadlines

Support the ability to sell others on the change initiative by providing them the facts and details they need to validate their message

Change Tips for Collaborators

When presenting the change message, don't exaggerate.

Validate the change message with facts and logic.

Admit when you don't know the answer; don't "wing it."

	Protector

Characteristics

Diplomatic and dependable

Good listeners

Can be indecisive in situations that involve change and risk

Contributions During Change

Loyal to organization and colleagues. When committed to an initiative willingly does back-stage work necessary to complete the task.

Provides insight on the potential affected of change on employees, clients, constituents, and other stakeholders.

Sensitive to the people side of doing business.

Needs During Change

Personal reassurance and sincere expression of appreciation

Clear instructions

Help with priorities and meeting deadlines

To be probed for their input and opinions

Change Tips for Protectors

Be more assertive. Speak up. Express your opinions.

Develop emotional boundaries.

Consider the benefits of change.

Try being more open to new ways of doing things.

	Initiator

Characteristics

Change drivers

Goal and action-oriented

Enjoy variety and an environment that is continuously changing

Push for speedy results and the bottom line

Contributions During Change

Business-focused and decisive, gets things done

Practical problem-solver

Works well in crisis, fast-paced, and turn-around situations

Needs During Change

Support in implementing change

Others to provide accurate data and details

Help with the people side of change

Answers to what are the costs? What will the solution do? How soon can it be done?

Change Tips for Initiators

Practice being more patient with those who hesitate to accept change.

Modify your expectations periodically.

Your high expectations may not be realistic for others who need more information and time. Others may find your approach pushy, become disillusioned, and lose motivation.

Questioner

Characteristics

Serious and industrious

Analytical and methodical

Objective and business-focused

Have difficulty accepting change unless they understand the purpose and rationale for it

Contributions During Change

Listens well and catches inconsistencies

Provide planning, organization, and structure

Keeps a keen eye on quality control and standards

Needs During Change

Ample time to make decisions

Limited surprises

Frequent communication with specifics

Help with indecisiveness and time management

Change Tips for Questioners

Practice being more flexible when applying rules and structure.

Try being more comfortable with and more optimistic about change.

Monitor your need for perfection.

During change, expect and accept time limits on data collecting and planning.

Discussion

Write two benefits each style brings to your change initiative.

Collaborator

_____

_____

_____

Protector

_____

_____

_____

Initiator

_____

_____

_____

Questioner

_____

_____

_____

Notes